All-New Cake Mix Magic

Publications International, Ltd.

Favorite Brand Name Recipes at www.fbnr.com

All photographs *except* those on pages 37, 53, 55, 71, 73, 75 and 91 by Stephen Hamilton Photographics, Inc., Chicago.

Photographers: Tate Hunt, Jennifer Marx
Photographers' Assistants: Daniel Ballesteros, Eric Coughlin
Prop Stylists: Thomas G. Hamilton, Paula Walters
Food Stylists: Kim Hartman, Kathy Joy, David Kennedy, Susie Skoog
Assistant Food Stylists: Elaine Funk, Thomas Sherman

Recipe Developers: Nancy Hughes, Sandra Johnson, Carol Wiley Lorente, Amanda Saxby, Sandra Wu

Pictured on the front cover: Mini Neopolitan Ice Cream Cake *(page 76).*
Pictured on the back cover *(clockwise from top):* Purse Cake *(page 58),* Lemon Poppy Seed Cupcakes *(page 48)* and Fruit-Layered Cheesecake Squares *(page 8).*

ISBN: 1-4127-2169-5

Manufactured in China.

8 7 6 5 4 3 2 1

table of contents

made from mixes

Fudgy Peanut-Coconut Candy Cookie Bars

Makes 24 bars

1	package (about 21 ounces) turtle brownie mix
½	cup vegetable oil
2	eggs
3	tablespoons water
1	cup peanut butter and milk chocolate chips*
1	cup semisweet chocolate chips
1⅓	cups flaked coconut
1	cup pecan pieces

Butterscotch chips may be substituted for the peanut butter and milk chocolate chips.

1. Preheat oven to 350°F. Grease 13×9-inch baking pan; set aside.

2. Combine brownie mix, oil, eggs and water in medium bowl; stir until well blended.

3. Spread batter evenly into prepared pan. Sprinkle with peanut butter and milk chocolate chips, semisweet chocolate chips, coconut and pecans. Press chips, coconut and pecans firmly into batter.

4. Bake 24 to 27 minutes or until toothpick inserted 2 inches from side of pan comes out almost clean. Cool completely in pan on wire rack. Cut into bars.

Fudgy Peanut-Coconut Candy Cookie Bars

Fruit-Layered Cheesecake Squares

Makes 16 servings

- 1 package (about 18 ounces) yellow cake mix
- ½ cup (1 stick) butter, softened
- 2 eggs
- 3 tablespoons water
- 2 packages (8 ounces each) cream cheese, softened
- 1 cup powdered sugar
- ¼ cup milk
- 2 teaspoons vanilla
- 1 can (8 ounces) pineapple tidbits, drained and juice reserved
- 3 tablespoons orange juice
- ¾ teaspoon cornstarch
- 1 medium banana (about 6 ounces), peeled and thinly sliced
- 1 cup fresh mango or nectarine pieces
- 1 pint whole strawberries, quartered

1. Preheat oven to 350°F. Grease 13×9-inch baking pan; set aside.

2. Beat cake mix, butter, eggs and water in large bowl 1 to 2 minutes on low speed of electric mixer or until stiff dough forms.

3. Press dough evenly onto bottom of prepared pan. Bake 27 minutes or until toothpick inserted into center comes out clean. Cool completely in pan on wire rack.

4. Meanwhile, beat cream cheese, sugar, milk and vanilla in medium bowl for 30 seconds on low speed of electric mixer until just blended. Beat 1 minute on high speed or until smooth. Cover and refrigerate until needed.

5. Combine reserved pineapple juice, orange juice and cornstarch in small saucepan. Stir until cornstarch is completely dissolved. Cook and stir over medium heat until mixture comes to a boil; cook and stir 1 minute. Remove from heat; cool completely.

6. Spread cream cheese mixture evenly over crust; arrange pineapple tidbits, banana slices, mango pieces and strawberries on top. Spoon or brush pineapple juice mixture over fruit.

7. Cover with plastic wrap; refrigerate 1 hour or up to 24 hours before serving.

Fruit-Layered Cheesecake Squares

Orange Coffee Cake with Streusel Topping

Makes 9 servings

- **1 package (about 19 ounces) cinnamon swirl muffin mix**
- **1 egg**
- **1 teaspoon grated orange peel**
- **¾ cup orange juice**
- **½ cup pecan pieces**
- **½ cup powdered sugar (optional)**
- **1 tablespoon milk (optional)**

1. Preheat oven to 400°F. Grease 9-inch square baking pan; set aside.

2. Place muffin mix in large bowl; break up any lumps. Add egg, orange peel and juice; stir until just moistened. (Batter will be slightly lumpy.)

3. Knead cinnamon swirl packet 10 seconds. Cut off 1 end of packet; squeeze contents over batter. Swirl into batter using knife or spatula. Do not mix in completely.

4. Spoon batter into prepared pan; sprinkle with topping packet and pecans. Bake 23 to 25 minutes or until toothpick inserted into center of cake comes out almost clean. Cool in pan on wire rack 15 minutes.

5. To prepare icing, if desired, combine powdered sugar and milk in small bowl; stir until smooth. Drizzle icing over top of cooled coffee cake.

Orange Coffee Cake with Streusel Topping

Banana Bread Waffles with Cinnamon Butter

Makes 4 servings

- ½ cup unsalted whipped butter, softened
- 2 tablespoons powdered sugar
- 2 teaspoons grated orange peel
- ¼ teaspoon ground cinnamon
- ¼ teaspoon vanilla
- 1 package (7 ounces) banana muffin mix
- ⅔ cup buttermilk
- 1 egg
  Nonstick cooking spray

1. Preheat waffle iron.

2. Combine butter, powdered sugar, orange peel, cinnamon and vanilla in small bowl; mix well. Set aside.

3. Combine muffin mix, buttermilk and egg in medium bowl; stir until just blended.

4. Spray waffle iron with cooking spray. Spoon ½ of batter (1 cup) onto waffle iron and cook according to manufacturer's directions. Repeat with remaining batter.

5. Spoon equal amounts butter mixture onto each waffle.

Banana Bread Waffles with Cinnamon Butter

Blondie Biscotti with Almonds

Makes about 34 biscotti

- 1 **cup slivered almonds**
- 1 **package (about 18 ounces) white cake mix**
- ⅔ **cup all-purpose flour**
- 2 **eggs**
- 3 **tablespoons melted butter, cooled slightly**
- 1 **teaspoon vanilla**
- 3 **tablespoons grated lemon peel**

1. Preheat oven to 350°F. Line baking sheet with parchment paper; set aside.

2. Place medium skillet over medium heat until hot. Add almonds and cook 1½ to 2 minutes or just until fragrant, stirring constantly. *Do not brown.* Set aside.

3. Beat cake mix, flour, eggs, butter and vanilla in large bowl 1 to 2 minutes on low speed of electric mixer or until well blended. Stir in almonds and lemon peel. Knead dough 7 to 8 times until ingredients are well blended.

4. Divide dough in half. Shape each half into 12×2×½-inch log; place logs 3 inches apart onto prepared baking sheet.

5. Bake 25 minutes or until toothpick inserted into center of logs comes out clean. Remove from oven to wire rack; cool on cookie sheet 25 minutes.

6. Remove biscotti logs to cutting board, peeling off parchment paper. Using serrated knife, cut each log diagonally into ½-inch slices. Place slices on cookie sheet; bake 10 minutes or until golden brown.

7. Remove biscotti to wire rack; cool completely. Store in airtight container.

Blondie Biscotti with Almonds

Chocolate Hazelnut Cookies

Makes 4 dozen cookies

- ½ **cup chopped pecans**
- 1 **package (8 ounces) cream cheese, softened**
- ½ **cup (1 stick) butter, softened**
- 1 **egg**
- 1 **package (about 18 ounces) devil's food cake mix**
- 1 **jar (12 ounces) chocolate hazelnut spread**
- ¼ **cup powdered sugar**

1. Preheat oven 350°F.

2. Place pecans in small resealable plastic bag. Using meat mallet or rolling pin, finely crush pecans. Place pecans in small skillet over medium high heat; toast pecans 1½ minutes or until browned, stirring constantly. Remove from heat and set aside.

3. Beat cream cheese and butter in medium bowl 30 seconds on low speed of electric mixer or until smooth. Add egg; beat on medium speed until well blended. Add cake mix; beat 2 minutes on low speed until mixture is smooth and resembles thick cookie dough. Stir in pecans.

4. Roll dough into 1-inch balls; spray palms lightly with cooking spray, if necessary, to make handling easier. Place balls 1 inch apart onto *ungreased* cookie sheets.

5. Bake 8 minutes. (Cookies will appear undercooked.) Cool on cookie sheets 5 minutes. Remove cookies to wire rack; cool completely.

6. Spoon 1 teaspoon chocolate hazelnut spread on top of each cookie; sprinkle with powdered sugar.

Chocolate Hazelnut Cookies

Chocolate Chip-Oat Cookies

Makes 4 dozen cookies

- 1 **package (about 18 ounces) yellow cake mix**
- 1 **teaspoon baking powder**
- ¾ **cup vegetable oil**
- 2 **eggs**
- 1 **teaspoon vanilla**
- 1 **cup uncooked old-fashioned oats**
- ¾ **cup semisweet chocolate chips**

1. Preheat oven to 350°F. Lightly grease cookie sheets or line with parchment paper.

2. Stir together cake mix and baking powder in large bowl. Add oil, eggs and vanilla; beat by hand until well blended. Stir in oats and chocolate chips.

3. Drop dough by slightly rounded tablespoonfuls 2 inches apart onto prepared cookie sheets. Bake 10 minutes or until golden brown. *Do not overbake.*

4. Cool on cookie sheets 5 minutes; remove to wire rack to cool completely.

Chocolate Chip-Oat Cookies

Zucchini-Orange Bread

Makes about 16 slices

 1 **package (about 17 ounces) cranberry-orange muffin mix**
1½ **cups shredded zucchini (about 6 ounces)**
 1 **cup water**
 1 **teaspoon ground cinnamon**
 1 **teaspoon grated orange peel (optional)**
  Cream cheese (optional)

1. Preheat oven 350°F. Grease 8×4×3-inch loaf pan; set aside.

2. Combine muffin mix, zucchini, water, cinnamon and orange peel, if desired, in medium bowl. Stir until just moistened. Spoon batter into prepared loaf pan; bake 40 minutes or until toothpick inserted into center comes out almost clean.

3. Cool in pan on wire rack 5 minutes. Remove bread from pan to wire rack; cool completely. Serve plain or with cream cheese, if desired.

Zucchini-Orange Bread

marvelous mix-ins

Honeyed Apricot Cake

Makes 12 servings

- 1 box (about 14 ounces) honey corn bread mix
- ½ cup ground blanched almonds*
- 1¼ cups milk
- 1 teaspoon almond extract
- ¼ cup chopped dried apricots
- 2 tablespoons butter
- ¼ cup honey
- ½ cup sliced almonds
- 1 can (15 ounces) apricot halves, drained

To grind almonds, place almonds in food processor fitted with metal blade; process using on/off pulsing action about 30 seconds or until fine crumbs form. Do not overprocess or almond meal will become almond butter.

1. Preheat oven to 350°F. Line bottom of baking sheet with foil. Grease bottom and sides of 9-inch springform pan; place pan on baking sheet.

2. Combine corn bread mix, milk, ground almonds and almond extract; stir until just blended. Stir in dried apricots; set aside.

3. Melt butter in small saucepan. Stir in honey until well blended; remove from heat. Pour honey mixture into prepared pan; swirl to distribute evenly. Sprinkle sliced almonds over honey mixture; arrange canned apricot halves on top.

4. Pour corn bread batter over apricots; smooth top with spatula. Bake 40 minutes or until toothpick inserted near center comes out clean.

5. Cool cake completely in pan on wire rack. Just before serving, invert cake onto serving plate.

Honeyed Apricot Cake

Panettone Cake with Almond Glaze and Mascarpone Cream

Makes 10 servings

CAKE
- ½ **cup pine nuts**
- ½ **cup golden raisins**
- ½ **cup currants**
- 1 **cup warm water, divided**
- 1 **package (about 18 ounces) lemon cake mix, plus ingredients to prepare mix**
- 1½ **teaspoons anise seeds**

MASCARPONE CREAM
- 1 **cup ricotta cheese**
- ½ **cup mascarpone cheese**
- ¼ **cup granulated sugar**

GLAZE
- ⅔ **cup powdered sugar**
- 1 **tablespoon milk**
- 1 **teaspoon almond or anise extract**

1. Preheat oven to 325°F. Grease and flour 10-inch Bundt pan; set aside.

2. Place pine nuts in small nonstick skillet over medium heat. Cook and stir 4 minutes until nuts are lightly browned. Cool; set aside.

3. Place raisins and currants in 2 separate small bowls; add ½ cup warm water to each bowl and let fruit stand 5 minutes.

4. Prepare cake according to package directions, using half of water called for on package. Stir in anise seeds. Drain raisins and currants. Stir pine nuts, raisins and currants into batter; pour into prepared pan. Bake about 40 minutes or until top is golden brown and toothpick inserted near center comes out clean. Cool cake in pan about 30 minutes. Invert onto wire rack; cool completely.

5. Meanwhile, beat ricotta, mascarpone and granulated sugar in medium bowl 1 minute on low speed of electric mixer or until light and fluffy. Cover and refrigerate until ready to serve.

6. Stir powdered sugar, milk and almond extract in small bowl until smooth. Add more milk, ½ teaspoon at a time, until desired consistency is reached.

7. Place sheets of waxed paper under wire rack. Spoon glaze over cake; let glaze set 20 minutes. Serve cake slices with mascarpone cream.

Panettone Cake with Almond Glaze and Mascarpone Cream

Apple-Walnut Glazed Spice Baby Cakes

Makes 12 cakes plus 2¼ cups caramel glaze

	All-purpose flour for dusting
1	**package (about 18 ounces) spice cake mix**
3	**eggs**
1⅓	**cups water, plus 3 tablespoons, divided**
⅓	**cup vegetable oil**
½	**teaspoon vanilla butter and nut flavoring***
¾	**cup chopped walnuts**
12	**ounces Granny Smith apples, peeled and cut into ½-inch cubes**
¼	**teaspoon ground cinnamon**
1	**jar (12 ounces) caramel ice cream topping**

Vanilla butter and nut flavoring is available in the baking section of most large supermarkets.

1. Preheat oven to 350°F. Lightly grease and flour 12 (1-cup) mini bundt pans.

2. Beat cake mix, 1⅓ cups water, eggs, oil and flavoring in large bowl 30 seconds on low speed of electric mixer. Beat 2 minutes at medium speed.

3. Spoon equal amounts of batter into prepared pans. Bake 25 minutes or until toothpick inserted near centers of cakes comes out almost clean. Cool in pans on wire rack 15 minutes. Carefully invert cakes from pans to wire rack; cool completely.

4. Meanwhile, place 12-inch skillet over medium high heat until hot. Add walnuts; cook 3 minutes or until walnuts are lightly browned, stirring frequently. Remove nuts to small bowl; set aside. In same skillet, combine apples, remaining 3 tablespoons water and cinnamon; cook and stir over medium-high heat 3 minutes or until apples are crisp-tender. Remove from heat; stir in walnuts and caramel topping. Spoon glaze over each cake.

Apple-Walnut Glazed Spice Baby Cakes

Mandarin Orange Tea Cake

Makes 16 servings

1 package (16 ounces) pound cake mix
½ cup plus 2 tablespoons orange juice, divided
2 eggs
¼ cup milk
1 can (15 ounces) mandarin orange segments in light syrup, drained
¾ cup powdered sugar
Grated peel of 1 orange

1. Preheat oven to 350°F. Grease 9-inch bundt pan.

2. Beat cake mix, ½ cup orange juice, eggs and milk in large bowl 2 minutes on medium speed of electric mixer or until light and fluffy. Fold in orange segments; pour batter into prepared pan.

3. Bake 45 minutes or until golden brown and toothpick inserted near center comes out clean. Cool in pan 15 minutes on wire rack. Invert cake onto wire rack; cool completely.

4. To prepare glaze, combine sugar, peel and remaining 2 tablespoons orange juice in small bowl; beat until smooth. Drizzle glaze over cake. Allow glaze to set about 5 minutes before serving.

Mandarin Orange Tea Cake

Chocolate Glazed Citrus Poppy Seed Cake

Makes 12 servings

    1 package (about 18 ounces) lemon cake mix
    ⅓ cup poppy seeds
    ⅓ cup milk
    3 eggs
    1 container (8 ounces) plain low-fat yogurt
    1 teaspoon freshly grated lemon peel
      Chocolate Citrus Glaze (recipe follows)

1. Heat oven to 350°F. Grease and flour 12-cup fluted tube pan or 10-inch tube pan.

2. Combine cake mix, poppy seeds, milk, eggs, yogurt and lemon peel in large bowl; beat until well blended. Pour batter into prepared pan.

3. Bake 40 to 45 minutes or until toothpick inserted in center comes out clean. Cool 20 minutes; remove from pan to wire rack. Cool completely.

4. Prepare Chocolate Citrus Glaze; spoon over cake, allowing glaze to run down sides.

Chocolate Citrus Glaze

    2 tablespoons butter or margarine
    2 tablespoons HERSHEY'®S Cocoa or HERSHEY'®S Dutch
      Processed Cocoa
    2 tablespoons water
    1 tablespoon orange-flavored liqueur (optional)
    ½ teaspoon orange extract
    1¼ to 1½ cups powdered sugar

Melt butter in small saucepan over medium heat; remove from heat. Stir in cocoa, water, liqueur, if desired, and orange extract. Whisk in 1¼ cups powdered sugar until smooth. If glaze is too thin, whisk in remaining ¼ cup powdered sugar. Use immediately.

Chocolate Glazed Citrus Poppy Seed Cake

Rocky Road Cake

Makes 16 servings

- **1 cup chopped walnuts or pecans or dry roasted peanuts**
- **1 package (about 18 ounces) devil's food cake mix**
- **1⅓ cups water**
- **3 eggs**
- **½ cup vegetable oil**
- **2 teaspoons instant coffee granules (optional)**
- **4 cups miniature marshmallows**
- **1 jar (16 ounces) hot fudge topping**

1. Preheat oven to 350°F. Grease bottom of 13×9-inch baking pan; set aside.

2. Place 10-inch skillet over medium high heat until hot. Add walnuts; cook 3 to 4 minutes or until just brown, stirring frequently. Remove from heat; set aside.

3. Beat cake mix, water, eggs, oil, and coffee granules, if desired, in large bowl 1 minute on low speed of electric mixer until well blended. Pour evenly into prepared pan.

4. Bake 33 minutes or until toothpick inserted into center comes out almost clean. Remove from oven to wire rack. Immediately sprinkle marshmallows and toasted walnuts evenly over cake. Let stand 15 minutes.

5. Meanwhile, heat fudge topping in microwave according to package directions. Drizzle evenly over cake. Cool completely.

Rocky Road Cake

Blueberry Cream Cheese Pound Cake

Makes 1 (9-inch) pound cake

> 1 package (16 ounces) pound cake mix, divided
> 1½ cups fresh blueberries
> 5 ounces cream cheese, softened
> 2 eggs
> ¾ cup milk
> Powdered sugar (optional)

1. Preheat oven to 350°F. Grease 9×5×2-inch loaf pan; set aside.

2. Place ¼ cup cake mix in medium bowl; add blueberries and toss until well coated. Set aside.

3. Beat cream cheese in large bowl 1 minute on medium speed of electric mixer until light and fluffy. Add eggs, one at a time, beating well after each addition.

4. Add remaining cake mix alternately with milk, beginning and ending with cake mix, beating well after each addition. Beat 1 minute on medium speed or until light and fluffy.

5. Fold blueberry mixture into batter; pour into prepared pan. Bake 55 to 60 minutes or until toothpick inserted into center comes out clean.

6. Cool in pan on wire rack 10 minutes. Remove cake to wire rack; cool completely. Sprinkle top with powdered sugar, if desired.

Blueberry Cream Cheese Pound Cake

Chocolate Streusel Cake

Makes 12 to 16 servings

STREUSEL

- 1 **package DUNCAN HINES® Moist Deluxe® Devil's Food Cake Mix, divided**
- 1 **cup finely chopped pecans**
- 2 **tablespoons brown sugar**
- 2 **teaspoons ground cinnamon**

CAKE

- 3 **eggs**
- 1⅓ **cups water**
- ½ **cup vegetable oil**

TOPPING

- 1 **container (8 ounces) frozen whipped topping, thawed**
- 3 **tablespoons sifted unsweetened cocoa powder**
  Chopped pecans for garnish (optional)
  Chocolate curls for garnish (optional)

1. Preheat oven to 350°F. Grease and flour 10-inch bundt pan.

2. For streusel, combine 2 tablespoons cake mix, 1 cup pecans, brown sugar and cinnamon. Set aside.

3. For cake, combine remaining cake mix, eggs, water and oil in large bowl. Beat at medium speed with electric mixer for 2 minutes. Pour two-thirds of batter into prepared pan. Sprinkle with reserved streusel. Pour remaining batter evenly over streusel. Bake at 350°F for 55 to 60 minutes or until toothpick inserted in center comes out clean. Cool in pan 25 minutes. Invert onto serving plate. Cool completely.

4. For topping, place whipped topping in medium bowl. Fold in cocoa until blended. Spread on cooled cake. Garnish with chopped pecans and chocolate curls, if desired. Refrigerate until ready to serve.

Tip: For chocolate curls, warm chocolate in microwave oven at HIGH (100% power) for 5 to 10 seconds. Make chocolate curls by holding a sharp vegetable peeler against the flat side of a chocolate block and bringing the blade toward you. Apply firm pressure for thicker, more open curls or light pressure for tighter curls.

Chocolate Streusel Cake

cupcake creations

White Chocolate Macadamia Cupcakes

Makes 20 cupcakes

- 1 package (about 18 ounces) white cake mix, plus ingredients to prepare mix
- 1 box (4-serving size) instant white chocolate pudding and pie filling mix
- ¾ cup chopped macadamia nuts
- 1 cup white chocolate chips
- 1 container (16 ounces) white frosting
- 1½ cups flaked coconut

1. Preheat oven to 350°F. Line 20 (2½-inch) muffin cups with paper baking cups.

2. Combine cake mix, ingredients to prepare mix, and pudding mix in large bowl. Beat according to package directions. Fold in nuts. Fill muffin cups ⅔ full with batter. Bake 18 to 20 minutes or until toothpick inserted in centers comes out clean. Cool in pan on wire rack 10 minutes. Remove from pan to wire rack; cool completely.

3. Meanwhile, toast coconut. Spread coconut on baking sheet; bake at 350°F 6 minutes, stirring several times. Cool completely.

4. Microwave chips in small microwavable bowl 2 minutes at HIGH (100% power), stirring every 30 seconds; cool slightly. Stir into frosting.

5. Frost cupcakes; dip tops into toasted coconut.

White Chocolate Macadamia Cupcakes

Carrot Cream Cheese Cupcakes

Makes 14 cupcakes

- 1 package (8 ounces) cream cheese, softened
- ¼ cup powdered sugar
- 2 cups grated carrots
- 2 tablespoons finely chopped candied ginger
- 1 package (about 18 ounces) spice cake mix, plus ingredients to prepare mix
- 1 container (16 ounces) cream cheese frosting
- 3 tablespoons maple syrup
  Orange peel strips for garnish (optional)

1. Preheat oven to 350°F. Line 14 (3½-inch) muffin cups with paper or foil liners.

2. Beat cream cheese and powdered sugar in large bowl at medium speed of electric mixer 1 minute or until light and fluffy. Cover and refrigerate until needed.

3. Prepare cake mix according to package directions. Fold in carrots and ginger.

4. Fill muffin cups ⅓ full with batter (about ¼ cup). Place 1 tablespoon cream cheese mixture in center of each cup. Fill with remaining batter (muffin cups should be ⅔ full).

5. Bake 25 to 28 minutes or until toothpick inserted into centers comes out clean. Cool in pan on wire rack 10 minutes. Remove from pan to wire rack; cool completely.

6. Mix frosting and maple syrup until well blended. Frost tops of cupcakes; decorate with orange peel, if desired.

Carrot Cream Cheese Cupcakes

Chocolate Cherry Cupcakes

Makes 22 cupcakes

- 1 **package (about 18 ounces) devil's food cake mix**
- 1⅓ **cups water**
- 3 **eggs**
- ½ **cup sour cream**
- ⅓ **cup oil**
- 1 **cup dried cherries**
- 1 **container (16 ounces) buttercream frosting, divided**
  Green food coloring
- 11 **maraschino cherries, stems removed and cherries cut in half**

1. Preheat oven to 350°F. Line 22 (2½-inch) muffin cups with paper liners.

2. Beat cake mix, water, eggs, sour cream and oil in large bowl 30 seconds at low speed of electric mixer until just blended. Beat on medium speed 2 minutes or until smooth. Fold in dried cherries.

3. Fill muffin cups ¾ full with batter. Bake 20 to 24 minutes or until toothpick inserted into centers comes out clean. Cool in pan on wire rack 10 minutes. Remove from pan to wire rack; cool completely.

4. Place ¼ cup frosting in small bowl with food coloring. Stir to combine; set aside.

5. Frost cupcakes with remaining white frosting. Place 1 cherry half, cut side down, onto each cupcake. Place green frosting in piping bag. Use writing and leaf tip to pipe a stem and leaf onto each cupcake.

Chocolate Cherry Cupcakes

Boston Cream Cupcakes

Makes 22 cupcakes

    1 **package (about 18 ounces) yellow cake mix, plus ingredients to prepare mix**
  ¼ **cup instant French vanilla pudding and pie filling mix**
    1 **cup cold milk**
    1 **container (16 ounces) dark chocolate frosting**

1. Prepare and bake cake mix according to package directions for cupcakes. Cool in pan on wire rack 10 minutes. Remove from pan to wire rack; cool completely.

2. Meanwhile, whisk together pudding mix and milk until well blended. Cover and refrigerate pudding.

3. Use tip of sharp knife to gently poke small hole into bottom of each cupcake. Place pudding in pastry bag fitted with small round pastry tip.*

4. Place tip inside hole at bottom of cupcake; gently squeeze bag to fill cupcake with pudding. Repeat with remaining cupcakes and pudding.

5. Place frosting in medium microwavable bowl. Microwave at HIGH (100% power) 30 seconds; stir. Frost tops of cupcakes.

You may substitute a plastic squeeze bottle with narrow dispensing tip for the pastry bag.

Boston Cream Cupcakes

Mini Tiramisu Cupcakes

Makes about 4 dozen cupcakes

- 1 **package (about 18 ounces) yellow cake mix, plus ingredients to prepare mix**
- 4 **teaspoons instant espresso powder, divided**
- 1 **cup warm water**
- 8 **ounces mascarpone cheese, softened**
- 1 **cup whipping cream**
- 3 **tablespoons powdered sugar**
  Chocolate sprinkles, chocolate shavings or cocoa powder for garnish (optional)

1. Preheat oven to 350°F. Grease 48 mini muffin cups or line with paper liners; set aside.

2. Prepare cake mix according to package directions, reducing oil to 2 tablespoons. Fill each muffin cup ⅔ full with batter. Bake 15 minutes or until toothpick inserted into centers comes out clean.

3. Remove cupcakes from pan to wire racks. Use toothpicks to poke a few holes in tops of cupcakes. Leave out overnight, uncovered, to dry.

4. At least 1 hour before serving, dissolve 3 teaspoons espresso powder in water. Carefully dip tops of cupcakes in espresso; return cupcakes to wire racks.

5. Beat mascarpone in medium bowl at medium speed of electric mixer until fluffy. If mascarpone separates, continue beating until it comes back together again. Transfer to another bowl; set aside.

6. Beat whipping cream, remaining 1 teaspoon espresso powder and powdered sugar at medium speed of electric mixer until stiff peaks form. Fold ¼ whipped cream mixture into mascarpone. Fold mascarpone mixture into remaining whipped cream until blended. Frost cupcake tops. Decorate cupcakes, if desired. Refrigerate until ready to serve.

Mini Tiramisu Cupcakes

Lemon Poppy Seed Cupcakes

Makes 19 cupcakes

- 1½ **packages (12 ounces) cream cheese, softened**
- 1½ **cups plus ⅓ cup powdered sugar, divided**
- 1 **package (about 18 ounces) lemon cake mix, plus ingredients to prepare mix**
- 1 **tablespoon poppy seeds**
  Grated peel and juice of 1 lemon
  Candied violets (optional)

1. Preheat oven to 350°F. Line 18 (2½-inch) muffin cups with paper baking cups.

2. Beat cream cheese and ⅓ cup powdered sugar in medium bowl 1 minute or until light and fluffy; set aside.

3. Combine cake mix according to package directions; stir in poppy seeds.

4. Place 2 tablespoons batter on bottom of each baking cup. Place 2 teaspoons cream cheese mixture in center; cover with another 2 tablespoons batter. Bake 22 to 24 minutes. Cool in pan on wire rack 10 minutes. Remove from pan to wire rack; cool completely.

5. In small bowl, combine remaining 1½ cups powdered sugar, lemon juice and peel. Either drizzle glaze over cupcakes or dip tops of cupcakes into glaze to cover completely. Top each cupcake with a single candied violet, if desired.

Lemon Poppy Seed Cupcakes

Fudgy Mocha Cupcakes with Chocolate Coffee Ganache

Makes 18 cupcakes

- 1 package (about 18 ounces) devil's food cake mix
- 1 package (4-serving size) instant chocolate fudge pudding and pie filling mix
- 1⅓ cups very strongly brewed coffee, cooled to room temperature
- 3 eggs
- ½ cup oil
- 6 ounces semisweet chocolate, finely chopped
- ½ cup whipping cream
- 2 teaspoons instant coffee granules
- ½ cup buttercream frosting

1. Preheat oven to 350°F. Line 18 (2½-inch) muffin cups with paper baking cups.

2. Combine cake mix, pudding mix, coffee, eggs and oil in large mixing bowl. Beat 2 minutes on medium speed of electric mixer until well blended. Fill muffin cups ⅔ full with batter. Bake 22 to 24 minutes or until toothpick inserted in centers comes out clean. Cool in pan on wire rack 10 minutes. Remove from pan to wire rack; cool completely.

3. To prepare ganache, place chocolate in small bowl. Heat cream and instant coffee in small saucepan over medium-low heat until bubbles appear around edges of pan. Pour mixture over chocolate; let stand about 2 minutes. Stir until chocolate mixture is smooth and shiny. Allow ganache to cool completely. (It will be slightly runny.)

4. Dip tops of cupcakes into chocolate ganache; smooth surface.

5. Place buttercream frosting in pastry bag fitted with small round pastry tip. Pipe letters onto cupcakes.

Fudgy Mocha Cupcakes with Chocolate Coffee Ganache

Spider Cupcakes

Makes 24 to 27 cupcakes

1 package (about 18 ounces) yellow or white cake mix
1 cup solid-pack pumpkin
¾ cup water
3 eggs
2 tablespoons oil
1 teaspoon ground cinnamon
1 teaspoon pumpkin pie spice*
   Orange food coloring
1 container (16 ounces) vanilla, cream cheese or caramel frosting
4 ounces semisweet chocolate
4 dozen black gumdrops

Substitute ½ teaspoon ground cinnamon, ¼ teaspoon ground ginger and ⅛ teaspoon each ground allspice and ground nutmeg for 1 teaspoon pumpkin pie spice.

1. Preheat oven to 350°F. Line 24 standard (2½-inch) muffin cups with paper baking liners, or spray with nonstick cooking spray.

2. Combine cake mix, pumpkin, water, eggs, oil, cinnamon and pumpkin pie spice in large bowl. Beat at medium speed of electric mixer 3 minutes or until well blended.

3. Spoon ¼ cup batter into each muffin cup. Bake 20 minutes or until toothpicks inserted into centers come out clean. Cool 10 minutes on wire rack. Remove cupcakes from pan; cool completely.

4. Add orange food coloring to frosting. Stir until well blended; adjust color as needed by adding additional food coloring 1 drop at a time, blending well after each addition. Frost cupcakes.

5. Place chocolate in small resealable plastic food storage bag. Microwave at MEDIUM (50% power) 40 seconds. Knead bag; microwave 30 seconds to 1 minute or until chocolate is melted. Knead bag until chocolate is smooth. Cut tiny corner off one end of bag. Drizzle chocolate in four or five concentric circles over top of cupcake. Immediately draw 6 to 8 lines from center to edges of cupcake with toothpick or knife at regular intervals to make web. Repeat with remaining cupcakes and chocolate.

6. For spider, place one gumdrop in center of web design on top of cupcake. Roll out another gumdrop with rolling pin. Slice thinly and roll into "legs." Place legs onto cupcake to complete spider. Repeat with remaining gumdrops and cupcakes.

Spider Cupcakes

Leprechaun Cupcakes

Makes 24 cupcakes

1 package (about 18 ounces) yellow or white cake mix plus ingredients to prepare mix

1 container (16 ounces) vanilla frosting

Orange and red gumdrops, assorted candies and decorator gels

1. Preheat oven to 350°F. Line 24 (2½-inch) muffin cups with paper liners. Prepare cake mix according to package directions. Spoon batter into prepared cups filling ⅔ full.

2. Bake 15 to 20 minutes or until toothpicks inserted into centers come out clean. Cool in pans on wire racks 10 minutes. Remove from pans to racks; cool completely.

3. For leprechaun hats, sideburns, beards and mouths, roll out large orange or red gumdrops on generously sugared surface. Trim pieces to look like hat, sideburns, beards and mouths as shown in photo. Pipe decorator gel over seam for hat band. Place candies on hat band as buckle and on face as eyes.

Leprechaun Cupcakes

kiddie
cakes

Individual Flower Pot Cakes

Makes 18 cakes

- 18 (2½×4-inch) sterilized unglazed terra cotta flower pots*
- 1 package (18 to 19 ounces) dark chocolate cake mix, plus ingredients to prepare mix
- 1 package (12 ounces) chocolate chips
- 8 to 10 chocolate sandwich cookies, broken
- 1 container (16 ounces) chocolate frosting
  Drinking straws
  Assorted candies: lollipops, gummy worms, spearmint leaf jelly candies
  Colored decorating icing (optional)

Wash and dry pots. Place in 350°F oven 3 hours to sterilize. Remove and cool.

1. Preheat oven to 350°F. Grease pots liberally and line bottoms with greased parchment paper.

2. Prepare cake mix as directed on package. Stir chocolate chips into batter.

3. Place pots in muffin cups; spoon batter into pots, filling ½ full. Bake for 35 to 40 minutes or until toothpick inserted into centers comes out clean. Remove pots from pan; place on wire rack to cool.

4. Frost tops of cakes with chocolate frosting. Place cookies in food processor; process using on/off pulsing action until coarse crumbs form. Spoon cookie crumbs on top of frosting to resemble dirt. Decorate with lollipop flowers**, spearmint leaves and gummy worms.

**Lollipop Flowers: Insert straws into each flower pot for "stems." Trim straws to different heights. Insert lollipops into straw stems. Pipe decorating icing onto lollipops to create petals and centers of flowers, if desired.

Individual Flower Pot Cakes

kiddie cakes

Purse Cake

Makes 1 cake

> 1 package (about 18 ounces) yellow cake mix, plus ingredients to prepare mix
> ½ cup seedless raspberry preserves
> 1 container (16 ounces) white frosting
> Red food coloring
> Assorted candies: black string licorice, licorice candies, black jelly beans, pastel egg sprinkles, candy bracelet, candy crayons

1. Preheat oven to 350°F. Grease and flour 13×9-inch cake pan; set aside.

2. Prepare cake mix according to package directions. Pour batter evenly into prepared pan. Bake 35 minutes or until toothpick inserted into center of cake comes out clean.

3. Cool in pan on wire rack 10 minutes. Remove cake from pan to wire rack; cool completely.

4. Use wooden picks to mark sections to be cut (Diagram A). Use serrated knife to cut cake into 4 sections. Discard ½-inch strip of excess cake.

5. Place widest section (Piece 1), cut side down, on cake board or serving platter. Spread left side of Piece 1 with preserves; attach next-widest section (Piece 2), cut side down, to the left of Piece 1 so layers are stacked sideways. Repeat process for remaining 2 sections. Final cake should gradually slope downward from right to left (Diagram B).

6. To make purse shape, measure 1 inch from side of shortest cake section. Using serrated knife, cut back to corner of tallest section. Repeat on other side of cake. Discard scraps (Diagram C). Cover cake with foil or plastic wrap and freeze several hours before frosting.

7. Tint frosting pink using red food coloring. Remove cake from freezer; frost cake on all sides.

8. To decorate cake, cut 18-inch piece black string licorice; gently press into frosting to outline purse flap. Cut ½-inch pieces to resemble stitching. Use 5 pink or white licorice candies to create flower petals. Place halved black jelly bean in center of each flower. Place pastel egg sprinkles in groups of 3 to add more texture. To make purse strap, knot 3 long pieces string licorice together. Braid licorice; knot other end. Push knots into frosting on sides of purse. Place candy crayons and bracelet around purse.

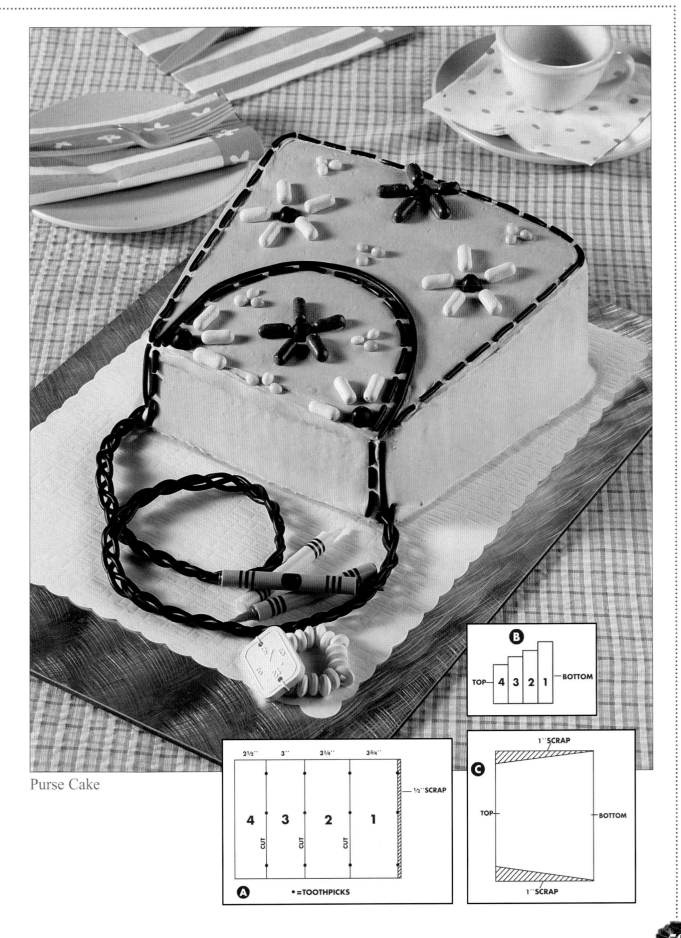

Purse Cake

B

TOP — 4 | 3 | 2 | 1 — BOTTOM

A

2½''	3''	3¼''	3¾''
4	3	2	1

— ½'' SCRAP

CUT   CUT   CUT

•=TOOTHPICKS

C

1'' SCRAP

TOP — | — BOTTOM

1'' SCRAP

Igloo Cake

Makes 1 cake

> 1 package (about 18 ounces) white cake mix plus ingredients to prepare mix
> 1 cup marshmallow cream
> 1 container (16 ounces) white frosting, divided
> 1 snack-size plain cake donut
> Blue food coloring
> White cake glitter
> Rock candy
> Plastic polar bear and penguin figurines (optional)

1. Preheat oven to 350°F. Grease and lightly flour 8-inch heatproof ceramic or metal mixing bowl.

2. Prepare cake mix according to package directions. Pour batter evenly into bowl. Bake 50 to 55 minutes or until wooden skewer inserted into center of cake comes out clean.

3. Cool in bowl on wire rack 10 minutes. Remove cake to wire rack; cool completely.

4. Using serrated knife, divide cake horizontally into 2 layers. Place bottom layer on serving plate.

5. Using long spatula lightly sprayed with cooking spray, spread marshmallow cream on bottom cake layer to within ½ inch of edge. Stack top cake layer on top.

6. Remove ¼ cup frosting from container; set aside. Use most of remaining frosting to frost cake. Attach donut to base of cake to form entrance to igloo; frost completely.

7. Color reserved frosting with blue food coloring and place in a pastry bag fitted with #7 plain tip. Pipe frosting in circular strips around cake, 2 inches apart. Pipe short, vertical strips between horizontal strips to give illusion of blocks of ice. Pipe doorway onto frosted donut.

8. Dust cake with cake glitter to resemble snow. Break chunks of rock candy and scatter around outside of cake. Decorate with plastic polar bear and penguin figurines, if desired.

Igloo Cake

Baby Doll Dress Cake

Makes 1 cake

> 1 **package (about 18 ounces) colorful sprinkle cake mix, plus ingredients to prepare mix**
> 1 **container (16 ounces) white frosting**
> **Assorted candies: strawberry licorice string, candy necklace, sour candy rounds and wedges, sour candy strips**

1. Preheat oven to 350°F. Grease and flour 13×9-inch cake pan; set aside.

2. Prepare cake mix according to package directions. Pour batter evenly into prepared pan. Bake 30 to 35 minutes or until toothpick inserted into center of cake comes out clean.

3. Cool in pan on wire rack 10 minutes; remove cake to wire rack. Cool completely.

4. Using toothpicks, measure and mark areas to cut (Diagram A). At top of cake, insert wooden picks 1 inch from sides. At 6 inches from top and 2½ inches from sides, insert 2 more wooden picks. Measure 4 inches from bottom and place 2 wooden picks at sides of cake. Using wooden picks as guides, cut away excess cake. Larger cake section is body of dress and cut-away sections will become sleeves and bottom of dress.

5. Place body of cake on serving plate. Position cake sections 4 and 5 for sleeves. Cut away about 4 inches from narrow end of sections 2 and 3 and position ends at hem end of dress, trimming to fit (Diagram B).

6. Secure sleeves and hem to dress using frosting. Frost top and sides of cake. Decorate cake with candies to resemble party dress.

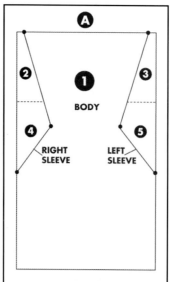

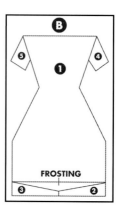

Baby Doll Dress Cake

Snail Cake

Makes 1 cake

- 1 package (about 18 ounces) yellow cake mix, plus ingredients to prepare mix
- 2 containers (12 ounces each) whipped cream cheese frosting
  Assorted food coloring: blue, green, yellow, red
- ⅓ cup seedless red raspberry preserves
  Assorted candy: Strawberry string licorice, candy-coated chocolate peanuts, chocolate pebbles, rock candy
- 10 gingersnaps, crushed

1. Preheat oven to 350°F. Grease and flour 2 (9-inch) round cake pans; set aside.

2. Prepare cake mix according to package directions; pour batter evenly into prepared pans.

3. Bake 30 minutes or until toothpick inserted into centers of cake comes out clean. Cool cakes in pans on wire rack 10 minutes. Remove cakes to wire rack; cool completely.

4. Spread jam on 1 cake layer; top with second layer. Looking down on cake, measure 6 inches from top of cake and using a serrated knife, cut across cake (Diagram A). Stand larger cake section (snail shell) upright on long serving plate. To keep serving plate neat, place long strips of waxed paper around perimeter of plate and slightly under cake. Tint 1 container frosting teal (blue with a hint of green) and frost snail shell. Add green food coloring to remaining teal frosting and place in pastry bag fitted with a #6 tip. Pipe swirl pattern on sides of shell.

5. Place half of frosting in remaining container in bowl; tint peach using yellow and red coloring.

6. Place remaining half-circle cake section on counter. Cut out snail's tail and head section. There will be scraps when forming head. Attach head and tail to shell and frost with peach-colored frosting (Diagram B).

7. Place a piece of strawberry licorice string on face to resemble a smiling mouth and 2 pieces for antennae. Use candy-coated chocolate peanuts for eyes.

8. Remove waxed paper. To decorate serving plate, spread a thin layer of remaining frosting on plate and sprinkle with ground cookies to resemble sand. Scatter with chocolate pebbles and rock candy.

Snail Cake

Juke Box Cake

Makes 1 cake

> 1 package (about 18 ounces) chocolate fudge cake mix, plus ingredients to prepare mix
> 1 container (16 ounces) butter cream frosting, divided
> Red and yellow food coloring
> 1 container (12 ounces) whipped milk chocolate frosting
> 1 tube (4¼ ounces) black decorating icing plus plain decorating tip

1. Preheat oven to 350°F. Grease and flour 13×9-inch cake pan; set aside.

2. Prepare cake mix according to package directions. Pour batter evenly into prepared pan. Bake 35 minutes or until toothpick inserted into center comes out clean.

3. Cool cake in pan on wire rack 10 minutes. Remove cake to wire rack; cool completely.

4. Meanwhile, prepare frosting. Place ¼ cup butter cream frosting in small bowl; tint red with red food coloring (about 20 drops). In another small bowl, tint ¼ cup butter cream frosting orange using 6 drops red and 8 drops yellow food coloring. Place each in pastry bag fitted with plain tips (#5 or 6) or resealable plastic food storage bag with 1 corner cut off.

5. Using paper plate as a guide, cut top of juke box into rounded shape. (Refer to diagram.)

6. Frost entire cake with chocolate frosting. Use some of remaining butter cream frosting to create semicircular background for records and wedge-shaped background for speakers. Using orange frosting, pipe small section above semicircle and grate on speaker section.

7. Place remaining butter cream frosting into pastry bag fitted with desired tip; pipe 2 panels between record area and speaker section.

8. Use black decorating icing fitted with plain decorating tip to add additional details.

9. Pipe red and orange stripes around edges of juke box.

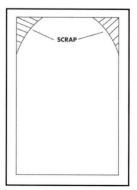

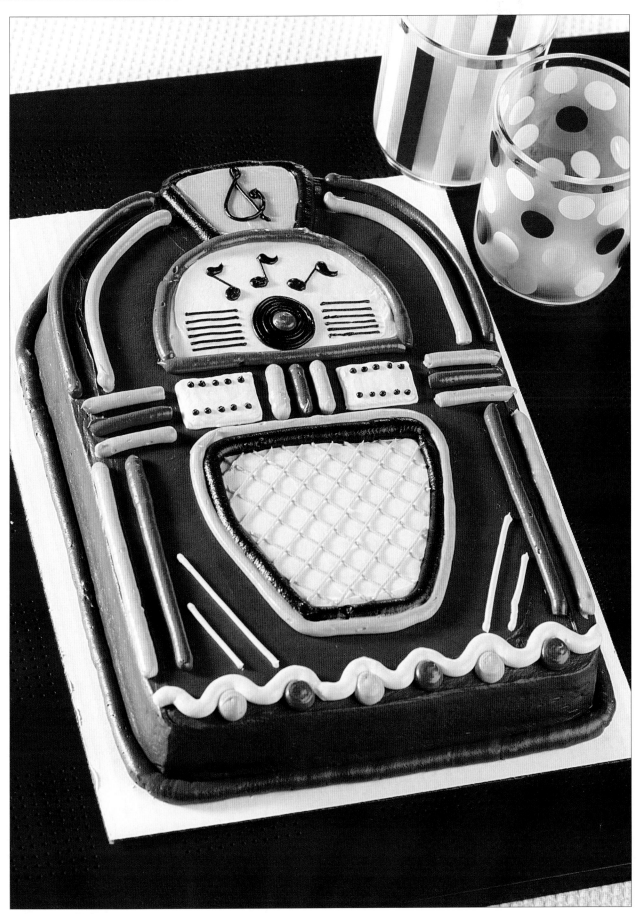

Juke Box Cake

Lighthouse Cake

Makes 1 cake

- 1 package (about 18 ounces) yellow cake mix, plus ingredients to prepare mix
- 2 containers (12 ounces each) whipped white frosting
- 1 tube (4¼ ounces) red decorating icing plus plain decorating tip
- 1 tube (4¼ ounces) yellow decorating icing plus plain decorating tip
- 8 vanilla wafer cookies
- 1 coconut-covered snack cake
- 1 foot-long strawberry fruit roll
  Assorted candies: sour candy rounds, red and orange licorice

1. Preheat oven to 350°F. Grease and flour 13×9-inch baking pan; set aside.

2. Prepare cake mix according to package directions. Pour batter evenly into pan.

3. Bake 35 minutes or until toothpick inserted into center of cake comes out clean. Cool in pan on wire rack 10 minutes. Remove cake to wire rack; cool completely.

4. Refer to Diagram A for cutting instructions. Place toothpicks in designated areas; cut away sections 1 through 4 and set aside. Trim ½ inch from flat side of sections 3 and 4 to fit top section of lighthouse.

5. Frost base of cake with frosting. Assemble sections (Diagram B); frost. Place cookies as indicated on diagram to resemble balcony.

6. To decorate, place strips of fruit roll diagonally across base of lighthouse. Use sour rounds for windows and licorice for door. Using decorator icing fitted with plain tip, pipe windows at top of lighthouse and lines onto cookie balcony. Place 1 snack cake at top of lighthouse. Cut orange licorice and place around snack cake to resemble light radiating from lighthouse.

x	TOOTHPICKS
----	CUTTING LINES
▨	CAKE SCRAPS

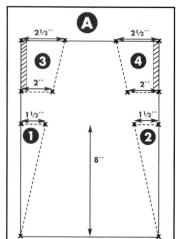

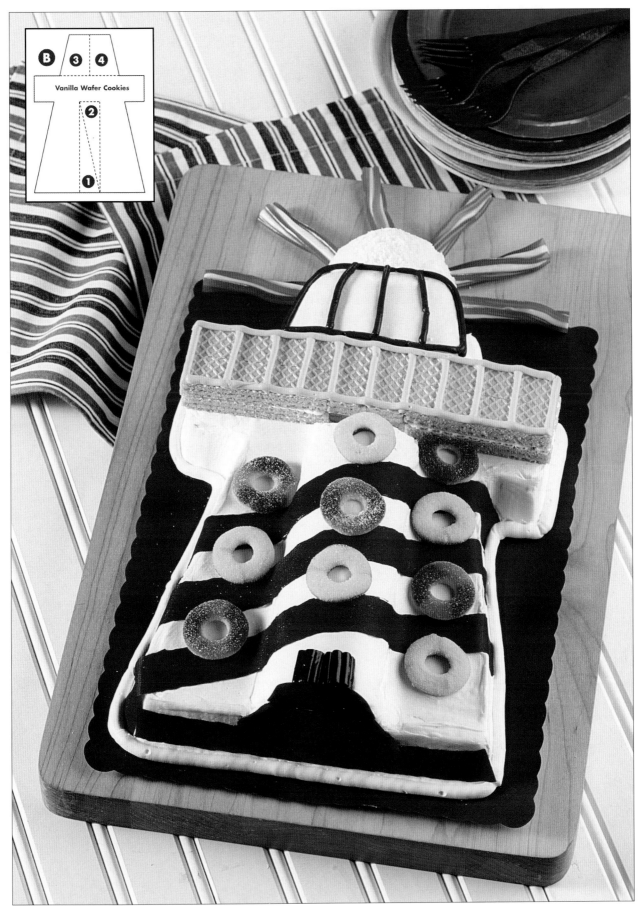

Vanilla Wafer Cookies

Lighthouse Cake

Back-To-School Pencil Cake

Makes 12 to 16 servings

> 1 package **DUNCAN HINES®** Moist Deluxe® Cake Mix (any flavor)
> 2 containers **DUNCAN HINES®** Creamy Home-Style Classic Vanilla Frosting, divided
> **Red and yellow food coloring**
> **Chocolate sprinkles**

1. Preheat oven to 350°F. Grease and flour 13×9×2-inch pan.

2. Prepare, bake and cool cake following package directions for basic recipe.

3. For frosting, tint 1 cup Vanilla frosting pink with red food coloring. Tint remaining frosting with yellow food coloring.

4. To assemble, cut cooled cake and arrange on large baking sheet or piece of sturdy cardboard as shown. Spread pink frosting on cake for eraser at one end and for wood at other end. Spread yellow frosting over remaining cake. Decorate with chocolate sprinkles for pencil tip and eraser band (see photo).

Tip: To make this cake even more special, reserve ¼ cup Vanilla frosting before tinting yellow. Place writing tip in decorating bag. Fill with frosting. Pipe name of child, teacher or school on pencil.

Back-To-School Pencil Cake

kiddie cakes

Enchanted Castle

Makes 14 to 16 servings

- 5½ **cups cake batter (1 package cake mix), divided**
- 1 **(15×15-inch) cake board, covered, or large platter**
- 2 **containers (16 ounces each) white frosting**
  Assorted food coloring
- 4 **sugar ice cream cones**
- 50 **chocolate-covered wafer cookies**
- 9 **squares dark chocolate mints**
  Assorted candies, decors and fruit rollups

1. Preheat oven to 350°F. Grease and flour 9-inch square cake pan and muffin pan. Pour 3½ cups cake batter into cake pan; pour remaining cake batter into muffin pan (¼ cup batter per muffin cup). Bake cake in pan 35 to 45 minutes and cupcakes about 20 minutes or until toothpick inserted into centers comes out clean. Cool 15 minutes in pans. Loosen edges; invert onto wire racks and cool completely.

2. Trim top and sides of square cake to even out. Slice rounded tops off 4 cupcakes. (Reserve remaining cupcakes for another use.) Place cake on prepared cake board. Place one cupcake upside down on each corner of cake, attaching with small amount of frosting.

3. Tint 1 container frosting pink. Divide second container frosting in half; tint half yellow and half purple.

4. Frost entire cake and cupcakes with pink frosting. Frost ice cream cones with yellow frosting.

5. Place frosted cones on top of cupcakes. Using medium writing tip and purple frosting, pipe decorative lines around tops and bottoms of cones, cupcakes and edges of square cake.

6. Place chocolate wafer cookies around sides of cake, alternating whole cookies with cookies cut down by one fourth to create castle wall. Decorate castle with assorted candies, cookies, decors and fruit rollups cut into flag shapes.

Enchanted Castle

simply elegant

Butterscotch Bundt Cake

Makes 12 to 16 servings

- 1 package (about 18 ounces) yellow cake mix
- 1 package (4-serving size) butterscotch-flavored instant pudding mix
- 1 cup water
- 3 eggs
- 2 teaspoons ground cinnamon
- ½ cup chopped pecans
  Powdered sugar (optional)

Preheat oven to 325°F. Spray 10-inch bundt pan with nonstick cooking spray. Combine all ingredients, except pecans and powdered sugar, in large bowl. Beat 2 minutes with electric mixer at medium-high speed until blended. Stir in pecans. Pour into prepared pan. Bake 40 to 50 minutes or until cake springs back when lightly touched. Cool on wire rack for 10 minutes. Invert cake onto serving plate. Cool completely. Sprinkle with powdered sugar, if desired.

Variation: Try substituting white cake mix for yellow cake mix, pistachio-flavored pudding mix for the butterscotch-flavored pudding mix and walnuts for pecans for a delicious Pistachio Bundt Cake with Walnuts.

Butterscotch Bundt Cake

Mini Neapolitan Ice Cream Cakes

Makes 4 cakes (12 servings)

Nonstick cooking spray
1 package (about 18 ounces) vanilla cake mix
¾ cup water
3 eggs
⅓ cup vegetable oil
⅓ cup cocoa powder
4 cups slightly softened strawberry ice cream
Cocoa powder, powdered sugar, strawberries and dark chocolate curls for garnish

1. Preheat oven to 350°F. Spray 4 (5¾×3¼×2-inch) mini-loaf pans with cooking spray; set aside.

2. Combine cake mix, water, eggs and oil in large bowl. Beat at low speed of electric mixer 30 seconds or until just blended. Beat 2 minutes at medium speed or until well blended, scraping side of bowl occasionally. Reserve 1¾ cups batter. Add cocoa to remaining batter; stir until well blended.

3. Divide chocolate batter evenly between 2 prepared pans. Divide reserved plain batter evenly between remaining 2 prepared pans.

4. Bake 30 minutes or until toothpicks inserted into centers come out clean. Cool in pans 10 minutes. Remove cakes from pans to wire racks; cool completely.

5. Trim rounded tops of cakes with long serrated knife; discard trimmings. Cut each cake in half horizontally. Line 4 clean mini-loaf pans with plastic wrap, leaving 2-inch overhang on all sides. Place 1 chocolate cake layer in each pan.

6. Place ice cream in large bowl; beat at medium speed about 30 seconds or just until spreadable. Spread 1 cup ice cream over each chocolate cake layer in pans; top with vanilla cake layers. Cover tops of cakes with plastic wrap. Freeze at least 4 hours.

7. Remove cakes from loaf pans. Remove plastic wrap; trim any uneven sides. Place 2 cakes vanilla side up; sprinkle lightly with cocoa powder. Place remaining 2 cakes chocolate side up; sprinkle lightly with powdered sugar. Garnish all 4 cakes with dark chocolate curls and sliced strawberries. To serve, cut each cake crosswise into 3 slices.

Mini Neapolitan Ice Cream Cakes

Dark Chocolate Lava Cakes

Makes 14 cakes

1½ **cups cold milk**
 1 **package (4-serving size) instant chocolate pudding and pie filling mix**
 1 **package (about 18 ounces) dark chocolate cake mix**
 1 **cup buttermilk**
 2 **whole eggs**
 3 **egg yolks**
 2 **tablespoons water**
 ¼ **cup vegetable oil**
 1 **tablespoon butter, melted**
 ¼ **cup granulated sugar**
   Sifted powdered sugar

1. Combine milk and pudding mix in medium bowl; whisk until smooth. Place plastic wrap on surface of pudding; refrigerate.

2. Combine cake mix, buttermilk, whole eggs, egg yolks, oil and water in large bowl; stir by hand until almost smooth (a few lumps will remain). *Do not use electric mixer.* Cover and refrigerate batter 1 hour.

3. Preheat oven to 400°F. Brush melted butter inside 14 (5-ounce) ramekins. Sprinkle evenly with granulated sugar.

4. Place 2 tablespoons batter into each prepared ramekin. Bake 10 to 12 minutes (batter will not cook through completely). Remove ramekins from oven; place 1 heaping tablespoon pudding in center of each ramekin and cover with 2 tablespoons batter.

5. Bake 14 to 16 minutes until wooden pick inserted in top layer of cakes comes out clean. Remove from oven to wire racks; cool 7 to 10 minutes. Invert cakes onto serving plates. Sprinkle with powdered sugar. Serve immediately.

Dark Chocolate Lava Cake

Coconut Mother's Day Cake

Makes 1 (8-inch) cake (10 servings)

- **1 package (about 18 ounces) white cake mix**
- **1 can (about 13 ounces) coconut milk**
- **4 egg whites**
- **1 container (16 ounces) vanilla frosting**
- **2 cups flaked coconut**
- **Violet food coloring paste**
- **Edible flowers (optional)**

1. Preheat oven to 350°F. Grease 2 (8-inch) round cake pans; line with with parchment paper.

2. Beat cake mix, coconut milk and egg whites in large bowl 30 seconds on low speed of electric mixer. Beat 2 minutes on medium-low speed or until well blended.

3. Divide batter evenly between prepared pans. Bake 40 to 45 minutes or until toothpick inserted in center comes out clean. Cool cakes in pans on wire racks 10 minutes. Remove cakes from pans to wire racks; cool completely.

4. Place 1 cake layer on cake board or serving platter; frost top with vanilla frosting. Top with remaining layer; frost side and top of cake with remaining frosting.

5. Place coconut in large resealable plastic food storage bag; use toothpick to add small amount of food coloring. Seal bag; knead until coconut is evenly tinted. Press coconut into frosting on side of cake. Garnish with flowers, if desired.

Coconut Mother's Day Cake

Tropical Bananas Foster Upside-Down Cake

Makes 1 (9-inch) cake (12 servings)

- 4 **tablespoons butter**
- 2 **tablespoons rum** *or* **1 teaspoon rum flavoring**
- ½ **cup packed brown sugar**
- 2 **large bananas, cut diagonally into ¼-inch pieces**
- 1 **package (about 18 ounces) banana walnut bread mix, plus ingredients to prepare mix**
- 1 **cup flaked coconut**
  Additional flaked coconut for garnish
  Vanilla ice cream (optional)

1. Preheat oven to 350°F. Line baking sheet with foil. Spray bottom and side of 9-inch springform pan with nonstick cooking spray. Place pan on baking sheet.

2. Melt butter in small saucepan over low heat. Add rum; cook and stir 2 minutes. Stir in sugar; remove from heat. Pour sugar mixture into prepared pan; swirl to coat bottom evenly. Arrange banana slices in even layer on sugar mixture.

3. Prepare bread mix according to package directions. Stir in coconut. Pour batter over banana slices.

4. Bake about 45 minutes or until wooden pick inserted in center comes out clean. Cool completely in pan on wire rack. Invert cake onto serving plate. Garnish with additional coconut and serve with vanilla ice cream, if desired.

Tropical Bananas Foster Upside-Down Cake

Raspberry-Orange Trifle with White Chocolate Custard

Makes 8 to 10 servings

- 1 package (16 ounces) pound cake mix, plus ingredients to prepare mix
- 1½ teaspoons orange extract
- 2 tablespoons sherry
- 1 package (4-serving size) white chocolate instant pudding mix, plus ingredients to prepare pudding
- 1 cup cold milk
- 1 cup red raspberry preserves or jam
  Red raspberries, kiwi slices or peach slices
  Whipped cream
  Blanched slivered almonds (optional)

1. Preheat oven to 350°F. Grease 9×5-inch loaf pan; set aside.

2. Prepare pound cake according to package directions; stir in orange extract. Bake in prepared pan according to package directions. Cool in pan 15 minutes. Remove cake from pan to wire rack; cool completely.

3. Trim off browned bottom, edges and top; discard. Cut cake into 1-inch cubes. Place cake cubes in large bowl; sprinkle with sherry. Set aside. Combine pudding mix and milk in medium bowl; whisk until smooth. Cover and refrigerate 30 minutes.

4. Just before serving, place raspberry preserves in microwavable bowl. Microwave on HIGH (100% power) 5 to 10 seconds or just until preserves can be stirred into a sauce.

5. Layer cake cubes, raspberry sauce, pudding and fruit in martini glasses or dessert dishes. Top with whipped cream; sprinkle with almonds, if desired.

Variation: Layer cake cubes, sauce, pudding and fruit in large glass serving bowl; top with whipped cream and almonds, if desired.

Tip: Trifle may be served immediately; however, flavors will develop and be more pronounced if dessert is prepared at least 2 hours before serving.

Raspberry-Orange Trifle with White Chocolate Custard

Almond Cake

Makes 1 (9-inch) cake (12 servings)

    1 can (8 ounces) almond paste
    3 eggs
    1 package (about 18 ounces) white cake mix
 1¼ cups water
    ⅓ cup vegetable oil
    1 container (12 ounces) whipped vanilla frosting
    1 tablespoon seedless raspberry preserves
      Candy-coated almonds for garnish

1. Preheat oven to 350°F. Grease 2 (9-inch) round cake pans. Line bottom of pans with parchment paper; spray parchment with nonstick cooking spray.

2. Place almond paste and eggs in large mixing bowl; stir until smooth and no lumps remain.

3. Add cake mix, water and oil to almond paste mixture. Beat 1 minute on low speed of electric mixer. Beat 2 minutes on medium-low or until well blended.

4. Divide batter evenly between cake pans. Bake 35 minutes or until wooden pick inserted into centers comes out clean. Cool completely in pans on wire racks; remove cakes from pans.

5. For filling, place ¼ cup frosting into small bowl; stir in preserves. Place 1 layer on serving plate. Spread filling onto top of layer to within ¼ inch of edge. Top with remaining layer. Frost sides and top of cake with remaining white frosting. Decorate with almonds.

Variation: Use ¼ cup seedless raspberry preserves instead of flavored frosting for filling.

Almond Cake

Chai Spice Cake
Makes 1 (9-inch) bundt cake (about 16 slices)

- 2¼ **cups water**
- 10 **chai tea bags**
- 1 **cup ice cubes**
- 1 **package (about 18 ounces) white cake mix**
- 3 **egg whites**
- ⅓ **cup vegetable oil**
- 1 **tablespoon cornstarch**
- ¼ **cup packed dark brown sugar**
- 6 **whole cloves**
- ½ **teaspoon vanilla**

1. Preheat oven to 350°F. Spray bottom only of nonstick tube pan or Bundt pan with nonstick cooking spray.

2. Bring water to a boil in medium saucepan over high heat. Remove from heat; add tea bags. Steep 5 minutes. Remove and discard tea bags from saucepan. Add ice cubes to tea; let stand until ice is completely melted. (This should make 2¼ cups tea.)

3. Beat cake mix, 1¼ cups tea, egg whites and oil 30 seconds on low speed of electric mixer. Beat 2 minutes at medium speed or until well blended. Pour batter into prepared pan. Bake according to package directions or until toothpick inserted near center comes out almost clean. Invert bundt pan onto wire rack; allow to stand 10 minutes before removing pan. Cool completely.

4. Meanwhile, combine remaining 1 cup tea and cornstarch in medium saucepan; stir until cornstarch is completely dissolved. Add sugar and cloves. Bring to a boil over medium-high heat, stirring constantly; boil 1 minute, stirring constantly. Remove from heat; cool completely. Discard cloves; stir in vanilla. Pour glaze evenly over cake.

Chai Spice Cake

Chocolate-Raspberry Layer Cake

Makes 8 to 10 servings

> 2 packages (about 18 ounces each) chocolate cake mix, plus ingredients to prepare mixes
> 1 jar (10 ounces) seedless red raspberry fruit spread, divided
> 1 package (12 ounces) white chocolate chips, divided
> 1 container (16 ounces) chocolate frosting
> ½ pint fresh raspberries
> 1 to 2 cups toasted sliced almonds

1. Preheat oven to 350°F. Grease and flour 4 (9-inch) round cake pans. Prepare cake batter according to package directions. Pour into prepared pans. Bake as directed on package. Cool completely.

2. Place one cake layer on serving plate. Spread with ⅓ of fruit spread. Sprinkle with ½ cup white chocolate chips.

3. Repeat with second and third cake layers, fruit spread and white chocolate chips.

4. Place fourth cake layer on top. Frost top and side of cake with chocolate frosting. Decorate cake in alternating concentric circles of raspberries and remaining ½ cup white chocolate chips. Press almonds against side of cake.

Chocolate-Raspberry Layer Cake

acknowledgments

The publisher would like to thank the companies and organizations listed below for the use of their recipes and photographs in this publication.

Duncan Hines® and Moist Deluxe® are registered trademarks of

Aurora Foods Inc.

Hershey Foods Corporation

index

index

index